BOBCATS

Henry Randall

PowerKiDS press.

New York

Published in 2011 by The Rosen Publishing Group, Inc.
29 East 21st Street, New York, NY 10010

First Edition

Editor: Joanne Randolph
Book Design: Ashley Burrell

Photo Credits: Cover, p. 24 (right) Shutterstock.com; p. 5 © Arco/H. Reinhard/age fotostock; pp. 6, 9, 24 (left) © www.iStockphoto.com/Tom Tietz; pp. 10, 24 (center right) Jupiterimages/Photos.com/Thinkstock; p. 13 © www.iStockphoto.com/Jeff Grabert; p. 14 Ralph Lee Hopkins/Getty Images; pp. 16–17 Comstock/Thinkstock; p. 19 © Corbis/age fotostock; p. 20 iStockphoto/Thinkstock; p. 23 Stockbyte/Thinkstock; p. 24 (center left) Corbis Visions of Nature.

Library of Congress Cataloging-in-Publication Data

Randall, Henry, 1972-
 Bobcats / by Henry Randall. — 1st ed.
     p. cm. — (Cats of the wild)
 Includes index.
 ISBN 978-1-4488-2520-2 (library binding) — ISBN 978-1-4488-2625-4 (pbk.) —
ISBN 978-1-4488-2626-1 (6-pack)
 1. Bobcat—Juvenile literature. I. Title.
 QL737.C23R354 2011
 599.75'36—dc22

                                        2010022367

Manufactured in the United States of America

CPSIA Compliance Information: Batch #WW11PK: For Further Information contact Rosen Publishing, New York, New York at 1-800-237-9932

Contents

This is a bobcat. This bobcat makes its home near the **mountains**.

Bobcats live in many places in North America. This bobcat has climbed a tree in its forest home.

Bobcats have long **hair** on their faces and the tips of their ears.

Bobcats have wide **paws**.
They help them walk on top
of the snow.

Bobcats have short **tails**. This kind of tail is called a bobbed tail.

Bobcats sleep in dens. This bobcat used a mountain cave as its den.

Bobcats are hunters.
They walk slowly and
quietly to get close
to animals.

Bobcats jump on animals they want to eat. They eat mostly rabbits and hares.

Bobcat babies are called kittens. They stay with their mothers for about eight months.

You now know a lot about bobcats. What else do you want to find out?

Words to Know

hair

mountains

paw

tail

Index

Web Sites

Due to the changing nature of Internet links, PowerKids Press has developed an online list of Web sites related to the subject of this book. This site is updated regularly. Please use this link to access the list:
www.powerkidslinks.com/cotw/bobcats/